Farm Poems

Selected by John Foster

First published in the United States of America in 2008 by
dingles & company
P.O. Box 508
Sea Girt, New Jersey 08750

First Printing

Website: www.dingles.com

E-mail: info@dingles.com

Library of Congress Catalog Card No.: 2007907145

ISBN: 978-1-59646-596-1 (library binding)
        978-1-59646-597-8 (paperback)

© Oxford University Press
This U.S. edition of *Farm Poems*, originally published in English in 1995, is published by arrangement with Oxford University Press.

Acknowledgments
The editor and publisher wish to thank the following who have kindly given permission for the use of copyright material:

Gina Douthwaite for "Milking Time", © Gina Douthwaite 1995
Richard Edwards for "The Cow in the Storm", © Richard Edwards 1995
Eric Finney for "Chicks" and "I'd Like to Be a Farmer",
both © Eric Finney 1995
Julie Holder for "The Tractor", © Julie Holder 1995
Richard James for "The Barn Owl", © Richard James 1995
Diane Johnson for "Growing Rice", © Diane Johnson 1995
Judith Nicholls for "Catch Them If You Can!", © Judith Nicholls 1995
Celia Warren for "Landscape Painting", © Celia Warren 1995

Illustrations by
Graham Round; Jackie East; Rachael O'Neill; Frank James; Lynda Murray;
Kay Widdowson; Jolyne Knox; Cliff Wright; Lisa Smith

Printed in China

dingles & company

I'd Like to Be a Farmer

I'd like to be a farmer
with animals to feed,
and a tractor to drive along
when I am sowing seed.

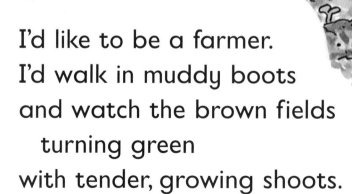

I'd like to be a farmer.
I'd walk in muddy boots
and watch the brown fields
  turning green
with tender, growing shoots.

2

I'd like to be a farmer.
After months of sun and rain
I'd drive a combine harvester
to cut the golden grain.

Eric Finney

Catch Them if You Can!

Chickens and hens,
chickens and hens!
Chicks in the farmyard,
chicks in the pens,
chicks in the kitchen,
under the chairs,
chicks on the doorstep,
chicks on the stairs . . .

Chickens and hens,
chickens and hens,
chicks in the farmyard
but NONE in the pens!

Judith Nicholls

The Cow in the Storm

The sky turned gray,
the horse went, "Neigh,"
but the cow just went on chewing.

The sky turned black,
the ducks went, "Quack,"
but the cow just went on chewing.

Lightning sparked,
the farm dogs barked,
but the cow just went on chewing.

Raindrops splashed,
the farm cats dashed,
but the cow just went on chewing.

Showers stopped,
rabbits hopped,
but the cow just went on chewing.

Sunshine streamed,
the whole farm steamed,
but the cow,
the cow,
the cow,
the cow,
but the cow just went on chewing.

Richard Edwards

The Tractor

The tractor is rough and ready
to do whatever it can.
It snorts and it chuffs and it roars,
and its wheels
are as tall as a man.
It clears the fields
of rocks and stumps.
It takes the trash
to landfills and dumps.

It plows the furrows
to plant the seed.
It takes the feed
to sheep in the snow.
Wherever you want
it will try to go.
The tractor is rough and ready
to do whatever it can.
It snorts and it chuffs and it roars,
and its wheels
are as tall as a man.

Julie Holder

Landscape Painting

Like a giant paintbrush
trailing up and down,
a tractor is turning the
field from green to brown.

Following the tractor,
greedy gulls in flight
look as if a pepper shaker
has spattered spots of white.

Celia Warren

Growing Rice

Rows and rows of families
in the hot sun
planting the rice
to feed everyone.

Rows and rows of families
in the hot sun
harvesting the rice
to feed everyone.

Diane Johnson

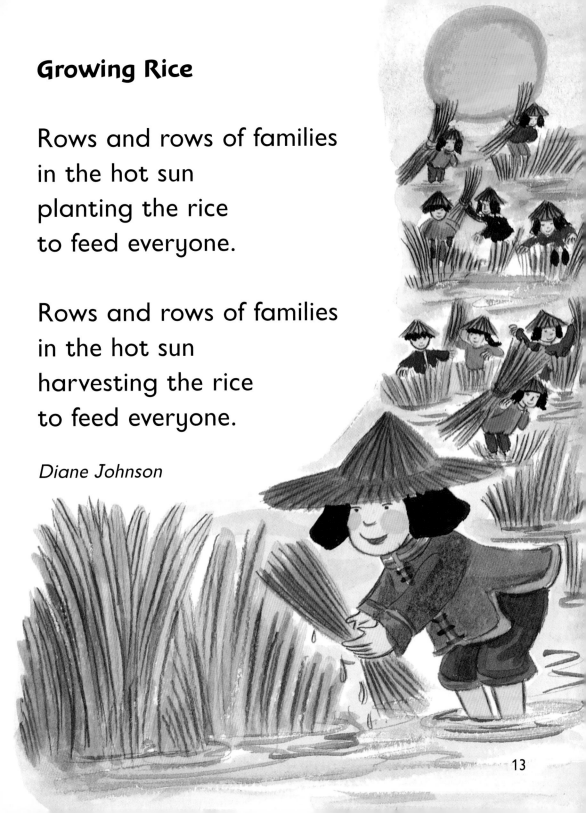

13

The Barn Owl

High up on the rafters
something white
sleeps in the shadows
waiting for the night.

High up from the rafters
something flies,
with silent wings
and big round eyes.

Richard James

Milking Time

Five o'clock in the morning.
Cows cross the dark yard
like white patches of jigsaw,
their hot breath making misty ghosts
in the crisp air.

Gina Douthwaite

Chicks

Yesterday
they were warm, brown eggs.
Now they're fluffy, yellow balls
on legs.

Eric Finney

16

Seasons Poems

Selected by John Foster

First published in the United States of America in 2008 by
dingles & company
P.O. Box 508
Sea Girt, New Jersey 08750

First Printing

Website: www.dingles.com

E-mail: info@dingles.com

Library of Congress Catalog Card No.: 2007907145

ISBN: 978-1-59646-596-1 (library binding)
978-1-59646-597-8 (paperback)

Acknowledgments
The editor and publisher wish to thank the following who have kindly given permission for the use of copyright material:

John Foster for "Harvesttime" and "One Summer Evening",
both © John Foster 1995
Julie Holder for "Seasons of Trees", © Julie Holder 1995
John Kitching for "Here and There", © John Kitching 1995
Wendy Larmont for "Winter Walk", © Wendy Larmont 1995
Tony Mitton for "Hibernating Hedgehog", © Tony Mitton 1995
Irene Rawnsley for "Footprints", © Irene Rawnsley 1995
Charles Thomson and John Foster for "You Can Tell It's Spring",
© Charles Thomson and John Foster 1995

Illustrations by
Beccy Blake; Claire Pound; Diana Catchpole; Jolyne Knox; Jane Gedye;
Jane Bottomly; Jan Lewis; Samantha Rugen

Printed in China

.·. dingles & company

Seasons of Trees

In spring
the trees
are a beautiful sight,
dressed in blossoms
pink and white.

In summer
the trees
are full of treats —
apples and pears
and cherries to eat.

18

In autumn
the trees
are red and gold,
and the leaves fall down
as the days grow cold.

In winter
the trees
are bare and plain,
waiting for spring
to dress them again.

Julie Holder

19

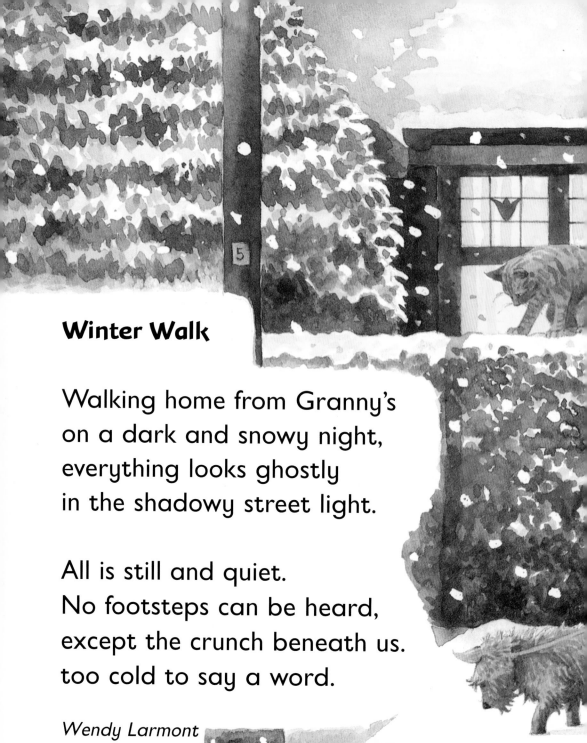

Winter Walk

Walking home from Granny's
on a dark and snowy night,
everything looks ghostly
in the shadowy street light.

All is still and quiet.
No footsteps can be heard,
except the crunch beneath us.
too cold to say a word.

Wendy Larmont

Footprints

In the winter
watch me go,
making footprints
in the snow.

In the spring
my boots are wet.
See how deep
the puddles get.

In the summer
by the sea,
sandy footprints
made by me.

In the autumn
trees are brown.
I kick the leaves
all over the town!

Irene Rawnsley

Here and There

There in Jamaica
the sun beats down.
Here the dark clouds
fiercely frown.

There in Jamaica,
bright blue, warm.
Here huge snowflakes
thickly swarm.

24

There in Jamaica
storms whip trees.
Here frozen ponds,
icy seas.

There in Jamaica,
a sun-tan glow.
Here wrapped up tight
from top to toe.

John Kitching

Harvesttime

Harvesttime! Harvesttime!
It's harvesttime again.
Time to cut the corn
and gather in the grain.

Harvesttime! Harvesttime!
Time to pick the fruits,
to gather in the nuts,
and dig up all the roots.

Harvesttime! Harvesttime!
In the autumn sun
We'll cut, pick, and dig
until the harvest's done.

John Foster

Hibernating Hedgehog

Here comes winter,
cold and gray.
The hedgehog tucks
itself away.

Here comes ice
and here comes snow.
It needs somewhere
warm to go.

28

Here comes mist
and freezing fog.
Here's a good old
hollow log.

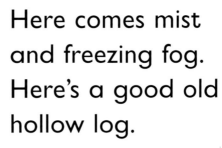

And here's a pile
of leaves that's deep.
It rolls up tight
and goes to sleep.

Tony Mitton

You Can Tell It's Spring

You can tell it's spring
when the trees turn green
and there are just puddles
where the snow has been.

You can tell it's spring
when the birds build nests
and Mom packs away
our warm winter vests.

30

You can tell it's spring
when the yellow heads
of daffodils dance
in the flower beds.

You can tell it's spring.
It's lighter each day,
and after school
we can stay out and play.

Charles Thomson and John Foster

One Summer Evening

We were playing catch
in the garden after school.
Dave dove for the ball,
but he missed
and fell into the pool!

John Foster